Junior Steps in RE

Year 3

MICHAEL KEENE
JAN KEENE

STANLEY THORNES

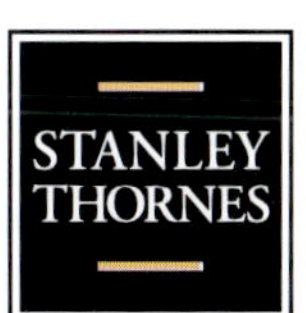

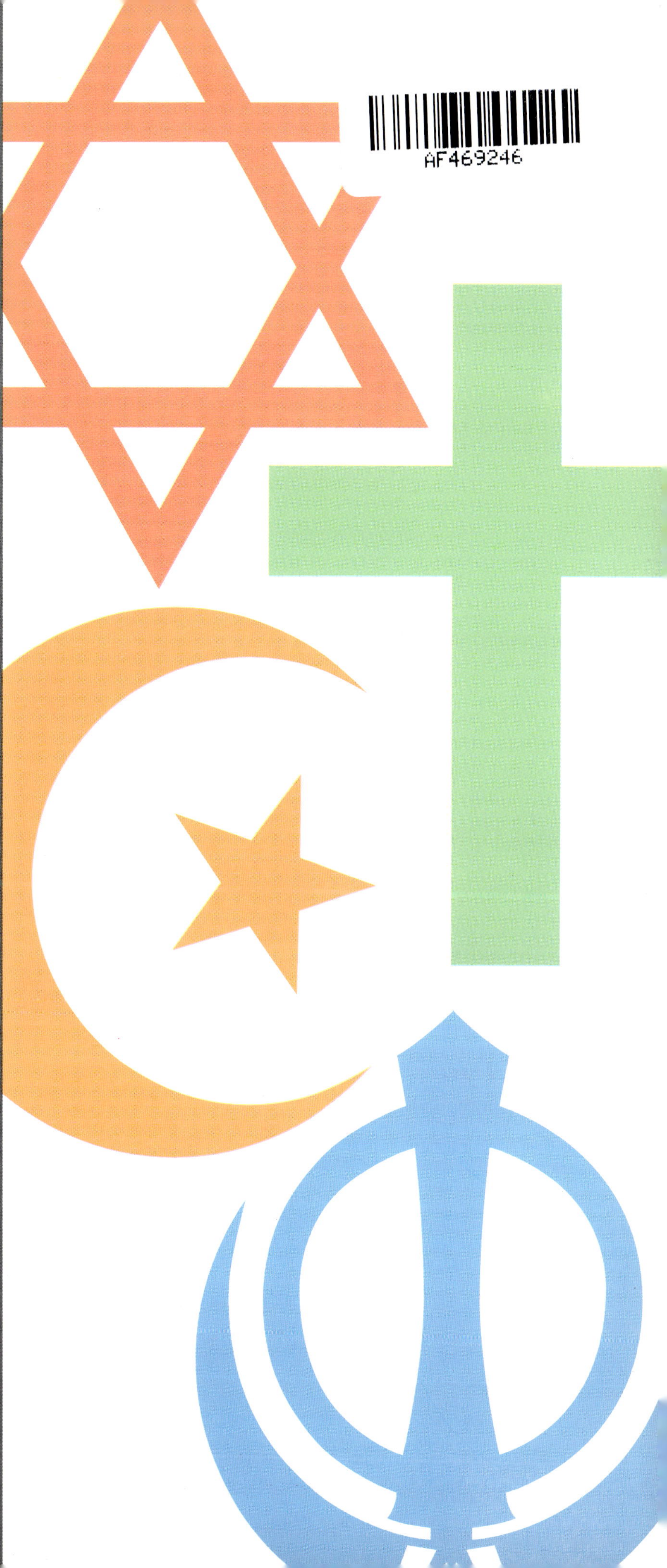

Acknowledgements
Artwork by Gillian Hunt © Stanley Thornes (Publishers) Ltd, 1996.
All photographs by The Walking Camera (Jo MacLennan and Alex Keene) with the following exceptions:
Blind person with dog © Collections/Fay Godwin; carved stone tomb in Petra, Jordan, Bedouin camel train, Muslims praying in the open air, Hinduism – Initiating the Sacred Thread Ceremony © C. Boulanger, all © Christine Osborne Pictures; Ka'bah at centre of mosque © SIPA Press, Rex Features; Mecca © Aral/Rex Features; Malaysian pilgrims travelling to Mecca © The Hutchison Library; Guru Nanak © Prodeepta Das; Enlightenment of Guru Nanak (detail) © CIRCA Photo Library.

First published by
Stanley Thornes (Publishers) Ltd
Ellenborough House
Wellington Street
CHELTENHAM
Glos. GL50 1YW

97 98 99 00 / 10 9 8 7 6 5 4 3 2 1

A catalogue record for this book is available from The British Library.

ISBN 0 7487 2100 2

Printed and bound in Hong Kong by Dah Hua Printing Co.

CONTENTS

LONG, LONG AGO

The **Torah** is a very old Jewish book. In it, there is a story that tells us how the world began. Everything in the world was made by God. God made the world in six days.

Day one
God made light and darkness. God called the light 'day'. The darkness was called 'night'.

Day two
God put a dome over the earth. The dome was called the 'sky'.

Day three
God put all the water in the world together. This was called the 'sea'. Dry land appeared. God called this the 'earth'. Plants and fruit-trees began to grow on the earth.

Day four
God put the sun in the sky. It lit up the sky each day. The moon and the stars gave some light at night.

Day five
God put fish in the sea. He made birds. They flew through the air.

Day six
God made every kind of animal. Then he made the first man and woman. He put them in a beautiful garden.

Day seven
God looked at everything he had made. He was very pleased with all his hard work. God rested.

IT'S A FACT

- **Judaism** is one of the oldest religions in the world.
- A person who believes in Judaism is called a **Jew**.
- The Jews have some very special books. The most important book is the Torah. This book is full of stories.

The Sabbath Day

Jews rest on the seventh day just like God did. This is called the **Sabbath Day**. On this day, Jews pray to God in special buildings, called **synagogues**.

WHAT DO YOU THINK?

Jews believe that God made everything. These photographs show two things that you know well. What are they?

THINGS TO DO

1. Make a diary for the week when God made the world. Draw a picture to show what was made on each day. Write a sentence about each picture. Use this book to help you.
2. Long ago, people thought the sky fitted over the earth like a dome. Why did they think this?

THE FIRST PEOPLE

The **Torah** (a very special Jewish book) tells us that God made the world in six days. It says that God made the first people on the sixth day. This is what he did:

First God made a man. God put him in a beautiful garden. There were trees, birds and animals in the garden. The man had lots to eat and look at. But he was very lonely.

So, God made a woman to be the man's best friend.

God told the man and the woman that they could eat fruit from the trees in the garden. But there was one tree that they must not touch.

God went away. Along came a snake. This was a bad snake. It could talk. It told the man and the woman to eat fruit from one of the trees. But it was the tree they had been told not to touch. The snake would not go away. In the end, the man and the woman gave in. They ate the fruit from the tree.

When God heard, he was very angry. The man and the woman tried to hide but he found them.

God punished the man and the woman.

WHAT DO YOU THINK?

Why do you think God was so angry with the man and the woman?

THINGS TO DO

1 Have you ever done anything wrong? What happened? Were you punished?

2 Make up a story about someone who does not do as they are told. What happens to them? Are they punished? Who by?

THE GREAT FLOOD

Soon there were many people living on the earth. But God wasn't very happy with them. They had become very wicked. So, God decided to punish them. He made up his mind to send a great flood.

But there was one man on the earth who was not wicked. His name was Noah. God did not want to kill Noah. He told Noah to build a big boat, called an Ark.

Noah's friends thought he was mad. They laughed at him. At last, Noah finished the Ark.

God told Noah to take two of every animal into the Ark with him and his family.

Then, it began to rain. It rained so hard that the land was covered with water. Everyone on the land died, and only Noah and his family were left alive.

After many days the rain stopped. Noah sent out a bird to see if the waters had gone. They had. He left the Ark with his family.

God was sorry for what he had done. So, he put a rainbow in the sky. This was to tell Noah and his family that he would not send another flood.

WHAT DO YOU THINK?

There were lots of animals in the Ark. What do you think it would be like to share your house with so many animals? What animals would you like to have in your house? What animals wouldn't you like to have at home? Why?

THINGS TO DO

1 Write the answers to these questions in your book:

- What does this photograph show?
- Have you ever seen a real rainbow? Where were you? Was it raining? Was the sun shining?
- Why did God put a rainbow in the sky?

2 Find out what colours are in a rainbow. List them in your book.

ABRAHAM

Abraham is very important to all **Jews**. They call him their father. He and his wife, Sarah, were the first Jews to live in Canaan. Canaan is called **Israel** today. Many Jews live there.

Abraham was born a very long time ago in a place called Ur. One day, God told Abraham that Abraham and Sarah should leave their home and go to Canaan. Canaan was a long way away, on the other side of a desert.

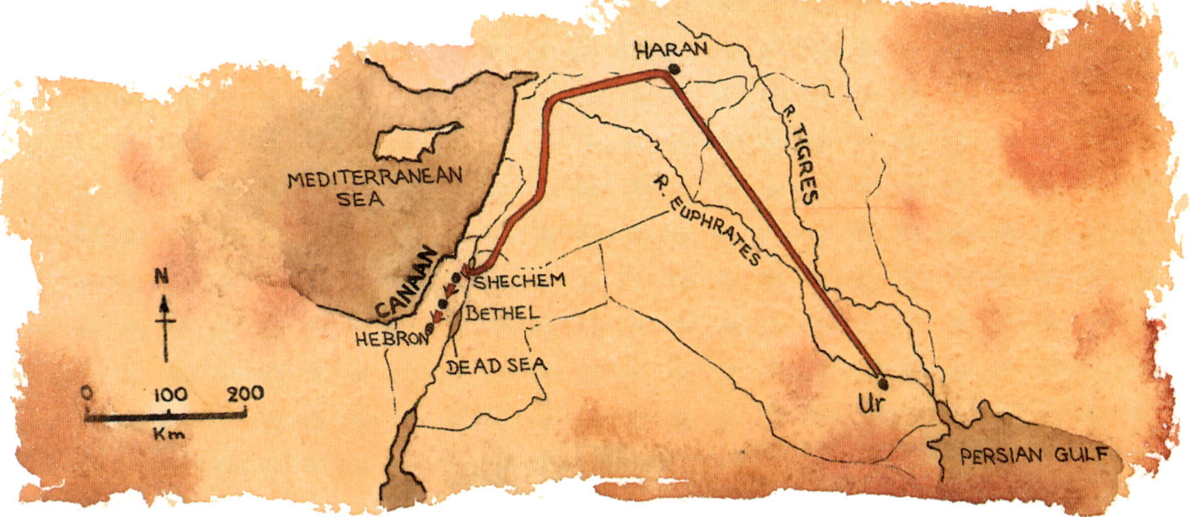

On the way to Canaan, Abraham and Sarah stopped in a place called Haran.

God spoke to Abraham. He told him to keep going. He said that Abraham could have all the land he found in Canaan.

Abraham and Sarah got to Canaan. They lived there until they were old. But there was one thing that made them unhappy. They had no children.

God promised that Sarah would have a child. She did. He was called Isaac.

Before he died, Abraham had many grandchildren. They all lived in the land of Canaan.

WHAT DO YOU THINK?

What do you think it would be like to travel across a desert in this way? Would it be hot? Would it be tiring?

THINGS TO DO

1. What would you need to take if you were going to travel across a desert? List five things.
2. Draw a picture of yourself going across a desert with your family.

SLAVERY

After **Abraham** and Sarah died, their family lived in Canaan for a long, long time. But in the end, they had to leave. There was no food to eat.

Many of the **Jews** went to Egypt to find food. When they got there, the leader of Egypt, the Pharaoh, made them work for him. The Jews were his slaves. For over 400 years, all the Jews born in Egypt were slaves.

Every day, the slaves had to make bricks for the Egyptians. The weather was very hot. It was very hard work.

God was not happy about what was happening to the Jews. He sent a brave man, **Moses**, to help them. Moses asked the Pharaoh to let the Jews go. But the Pharaoh kept changing his mind. First he would let them go, then he wouldn't. God was very angry about this. He decided to make the Pharaoh let the Jews go.

God sent horrible plagues to Egypt:

- The water turned to blood.
- There was no light.
- Many people had horrible boils.
- There were frogs everywhere.

In the end, the Pharaoh let the Jews go.
Moses and the Jews left Egypt. They started to walk towards Canaan. It took them many years to get there, and lots of people died on the way. This journey is called the **Exodus**.

WHAT DO YOU THINK?

Imagine that you were living in Egypt when God sent the plagues. What do you think it would have been like? Would you have been scared? Why?

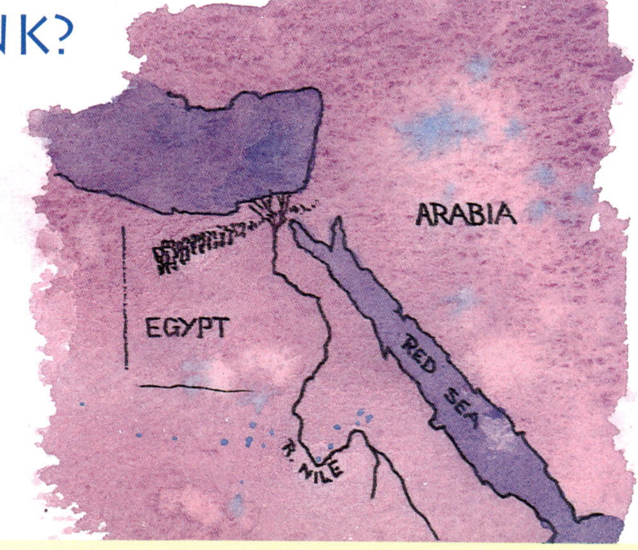

THINGS TO DO

1 Each year, Jewish people do something special to remember the Exodus. Find out what they do. You may need to ask your teacher for help.

2

This drawing shows the Jews walking across the desert to Canaan. Answer these questions:

- Which country were they leaving?
- What had they been doing in that country?
- How did God help them to get out of that country?

3 Imagine that you were a Jewish slave leaving Egypt. How would you feel? What happens to you?

THE TEN SAYINGS

It was a very long way from Egypt to Canaan. The **Jews** found it hard to keep going. They were very tired. The water they found to drink was horrible. They always felt hungry. People started to moan. **Moses** was very worried. He asked God what he should do.

God told Moses to throw a branch into drinking water.

It made the water taste good.

God told Moses that food would come down from the sky each morning. It did. The people were happy again.

But the people were still tired. They stopped to rest. They built a camp at the bottom of a mountain. Moses left the people. He went up the mountain by himself. He wanted to talk to God. God gave Moses the **Ten Sayings**, written on two blocks of stone. They told the Jewish people what they should and should not do.

WHAT DO YOU THINK?

The Jews were a very large group of people. There were thousands of them. Why do you think they needed some rules to live by?

Can you think of:
a) Five rules in your home.
b) Five rules in your school.
Who makes these rules? Why do you think we all need rules at home and in school? What do you think would happen if there were no rules in these two places? Would you like to be in a home or a school with no rules?

THINGS TO DO

Imagine that you were one of the Jews travelling with Moses. Think of three rules which might help everyone to live happily with everyone else.

JESUS IS BORN

Mary was a young Jewish woman. She lived about 2000 years ago in a town called **Nazareth**, in a country called **Palestine**. At this time, the Romans ruled over Palestine. One day, the **Angel** Gabriel told Mary that she was going to have a very special baby. The baby would be God's son. He would be called **Jesus**.

At the same time, the Romans decided to count all the people in the country. They told everyone to go back to the place where they were born. Mary, and **Joseph**, her husband, had to go back to **Bethlehem**. Bethlehem was a small village near **Jerusalem**.

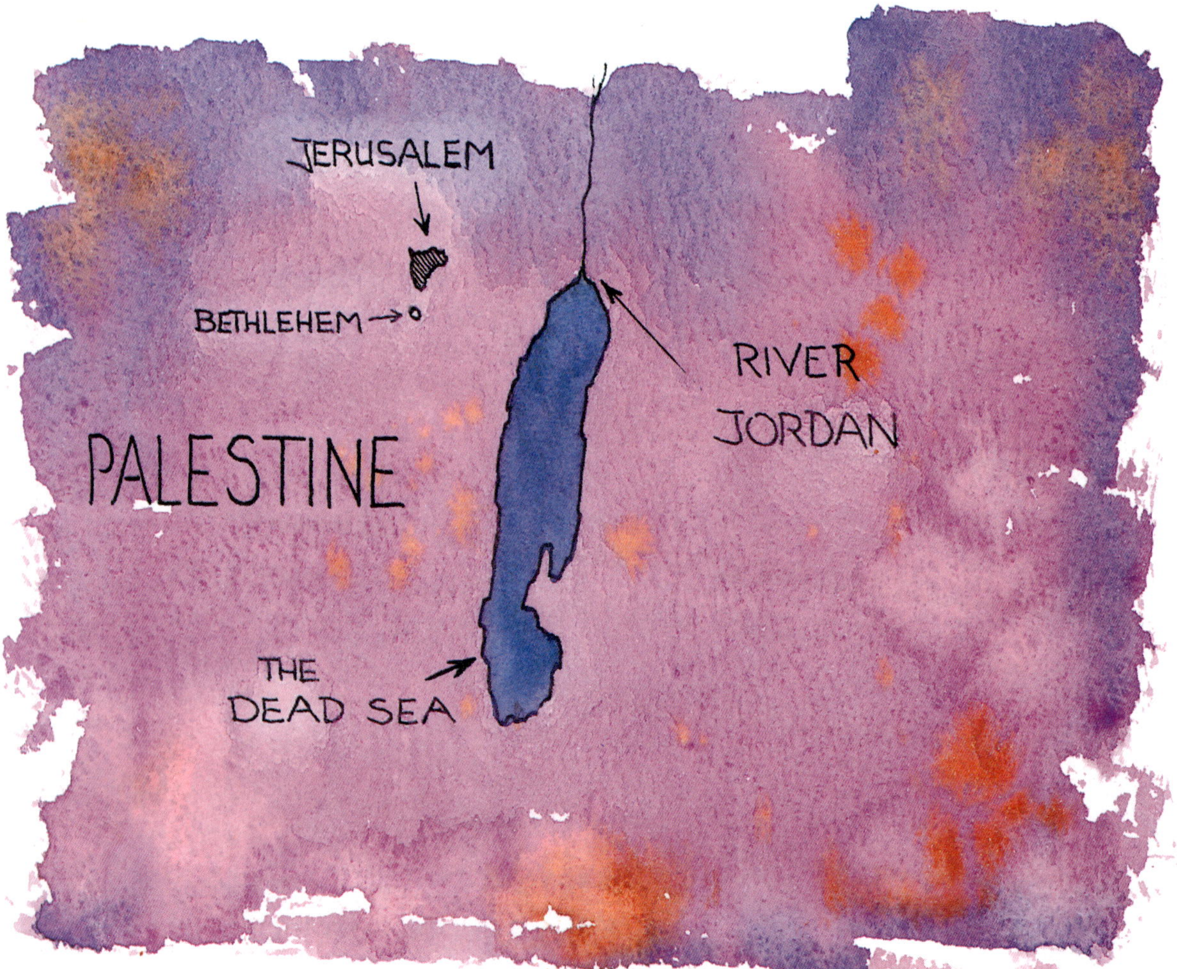

Mary and Joseph got to Bethlehem just before Mary's baby was born. At first, Joseph could not find anywhere for them to stay. But in the end they found a stable to sleep in. The baby Jesus was born in the stable, in a manger.

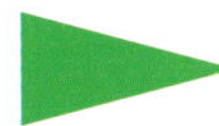

IT'S A FACT

The Romans ruled over Palestine 2000 years ago.

WHAT DO YOU THINK?

- What do you think it was like inside the stable?
- What would it be like to stay in a place where animals lived?

THINGS TO DO

1. Cribs show us what it was like inside the stable where Jesus was born. They show us who came to see the baby Jesus. Can you find Mary, Joseph and Jesus? Find out who the other people are.

2. Draw your own picture of Mary, Joseph and Jesus in the stable.

JESUS GROWS UP

Jesus grew up just like any other little boy. When he was 12 years old, he went to **Jerusalem** for the first time with his parents. They went to Jerusalem for **Passover**. Passover is a special Jewish festival.

Jerusalem was a big, busy city. People had come from all around to celebrate Passover. It was easy to get lost in the crowds.

When the festival ended Mary and Joseph left Jerusalem. It was so busy that they did not notice that Jesus was not with them. When they did notice they rushed back. It took them three days to find Jesus.

Mary and Joseph found Jesus in the **Temple**. He was talking to some Jewish teachers, called **scribes**. Jesus was asking them some very difficult questions about the Jewish religion.

Mary and Joseph were very upset and cross with Jesus. But Jesus said they should not be angry. He told them that he was doing God's work. He had been sent to earth to do this work, and nothing would stop him from doing it. Nothing must be allowed to get in the way.

IT'S A FACT

The Temple

The Temple was the Jewish place of worship in Jerusalem. Many teachers sat there teaching their **disciples**. The Romans pulled it down a few years after Jesus died.

The Barmitzvah

- When Jesus was alive, every Jewish boy became a grown up at the age of 12. There was a special ceremony to celebrate this.
- Today this ceremony is called a 'barmitzvah'.
- Now, Jewish boys have their barmitzvahs when they are 13.

WHAT DO YOU THINK?

- How long did it take Mary and Joseph to find Jesus? Do you think this was a long time for him to be missing?
- Why do you think they were cross and upset when they found him?
- Have you ever been lost? Were your parents very worried? How did they find you?

JOHN BAPTISES JESUS

John the Baptist was **Jesus**' cousin. John lived in the desert and only ate locusts and wild honey. He wore a coat made of camel's hair.

Locusts are large, flying insects. A large group of them will eat everything in a field in a few minutes. Some people cook and eat them.

John began to preach (tell people about God) beside the River Jordan. He told the people that God would forgive them for all the bad things they had done. But first they must be **baptised** in the river. This would show that God washed their sins away.

Jesus asked John to baptise him.

Jesus looked up and saw God's **Holy Spirit**. It looked like a dove. God spoke to Jesus.

He said that Jesus was his son, and he loved him very much.

IT'S A FACT

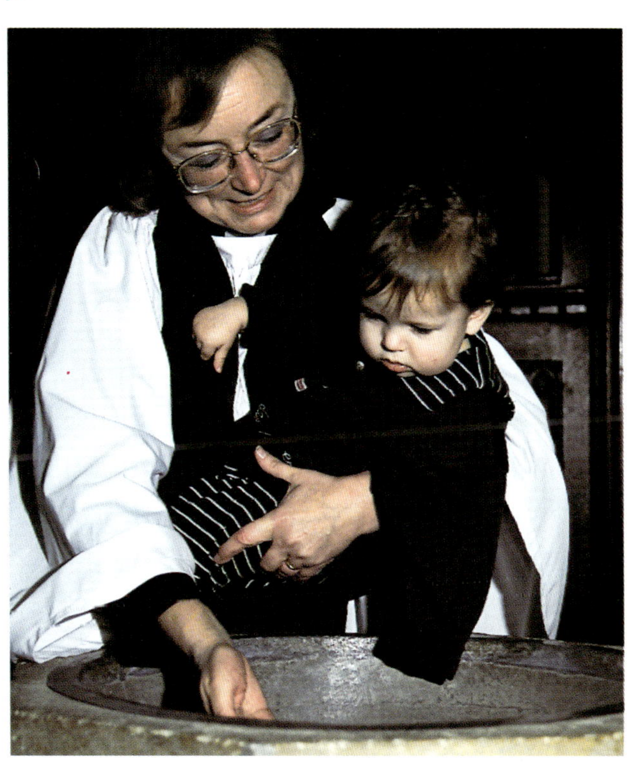

- Today, most people are baptised in church.
- Most people are baptised when they are babies.
- The Baptist Church baptises people when they grow up.

THINGS TO DO

1. Write down the two things that happened when Jesus was being baptised.
2. When are most people baptised? Were you baptised? If you have a baptismal certificate at home, bring it in to show to everyone in your class. Ask your mum or dad about what happened.

JESUS IN THE DESERT

Can you imagine what it would be like to live in the desert? When **Jesus** was alive, people believed that wild animals and evil spirits lived in the desert. Most people were too afraid to go there, but not Jesus.

Jesus lived in the desert for forty days. He was trying to decide what to do with his life. The **Devil** found him. He tried to make Jesus do some bad things.

Temptation One

Jesus had not eaten anything for a long time. The Devil told him to turn some of the stones into bread. But Jesus said no. He knew that he should not use God's power in this way.

Temptation Two

Then, the Devil told Jesus to jump from the top of the **Temple** building in **Jerusalem**. God would keep him safe. Then everyone would be amazed and would follow Jesus. But Jesus knew this was also wrong and said no again.

Temptation Three

After that, the Devil said that he could make Jesus the most powerful man on earth. Imagine that! But Jesus did not want this, and said no to the Devil.

The Devil could not make Jesus do any bad things, so he went away. Then, Jesus left the desert. He had decided that he must spend his life doing what God wanted him to. First, he had an important job to do. He had to choose some special friends – **disciples**.

WHAT DO YOU THINK?

Imagine that you had lived when Jesus was alive. Do you think you would have gone into the desert or would you have been too scared? What was there to be afraid of?

THINGS TO DO

Here is a list of words.

hot, dusty, cool, green, yellow, sandy, sunny, water, food, friendly, busy, empty

1 Which of the words do you think describe life in the desert?

2 Make up two sentences about what it would be like to live in the desert. Use a word from the list in each sentence.

JESUS CHOOSES HIS FRIENDS

Jesus had decided that he needed some special friends – **disciples** – to help him do God's work. He set off to find some.

Jesus met his first two disciples on the Sea of Galilee. They were fishermen called Simon Peter and Andrew, and they were brothers. Jesus asked them to go with him, to be his disciples. They set off with Jesus at once. Simon Peter became the leader of the disciples.

James and John were brothers and fishermen too. They were sitting in their boat when Jesus asked them to be disciples. At once, they climbed out of their boat, left their nets behind and went with Jesus.

Matthew was Jesus' next disciple. He collected taxes for the Romans. This made him very rich, but everyone hated him. Many people were surprised when he became a disciple. Jesus chose twelve disciples in all. They gave up everything to be with Jesus. They went everywhere with him.

Names

Do you have a nickname? Find out what your name or nickname means. (You may need to ask your teacher for help to do this.) Jesus gave some of his disciples nicknames. He called Simon 'Peter' – which means the rock. He called James and John 'Boanerges' – this name means the sons of thunder.

WHAT DO YOU THINK?

People everywhere need friends – just like Jesus did.

- Why do you like being with your friends?
- Why do you think that Jesus needed twelve special friends?

THINGS TO DO

Imagine that you are Peter, Andrew, James or John. You have been a fisherman for a long time and you really like it. One morning, Jesus comes to you and asks you to be one of his disciples. Write about what you would do. Would you go away with Jesus? What would you try to do before you went?

MAKING THE BLIND MAN SEE

Jesus and his **disciples** went to many places. Wherever they went, they helped people.

One day, Jesus was leaving the city of Jericho. A large crowd of people were with him. They walked past a blind beggar called Bartimaeus. Bartimaeus was sitting by the road, asking people for money or food.

Bartimaeus thought that Jesus might help him. He called out to Jesus but the other people told him to shut up. He did not want to. He called out even louder. Jesus heard Bartimaeus calling. He sent someone to bring Bartimaeus to him.

Jesus asked Bartimaeus 'What would you like me to do for you?' Bartimaeus answered at once. He said he wanted to see again.

Suddenly he could see again. Jesus said that God had made him well. Bartimaeus was so excited. He told everyone about the good thing that Jesus had done.

IT'S A FACT

- There are millions of blind people in the world today.
- In poor countries, little is done to help them.
- In this country many blind people have guide-dogs to help them.
- It is very difficult being blind in a busy city.

THINGS TO DO

1. Imagine that you went blind. What three things would you miss most of all? Why would you miss them?
2. Find out what your friend would miss. Would you miss the same things?

JESUS HELPS HIS DISCIPLES

There are lots of stories about the amazing things that **Jesus** did. This story tells us about a time when Jesus stopped a storm to save his **disciples'** lives.

Jesus and his disciples were sailing across the Sea of Galilee in a boat. Jesus was fast asleep in the back of the boat. He was very tired. He had been teaching and helping people all day.

Suddenly, a storm blew up. Big waves began to come over the side of the boat.

The disciples were very scared. They shook Jesus to wake him up.

Jesus stood up in the boat and spoke to the wind and the waves. He told the wind to stop blowing and the waves to calm down. They did.

Then, Jesus spoke to his disciples. He asked them why they had been scared. Didn't they know he would save them? The disciples could not think of anything to say. They had never met anyone who could do such amazing things before.

WHAT DO YOU THINK?

A coward is someone who gets scared very easily. Would you like to be called a coward? Do you think that the disciples were cowards? Would you have been scared if you had been in the boat with them?

THINGS TO DO

1 Look at this photograph. It shows a storm at sea. What do you think it would be like to be in a boat in this storm? Would you be scared?

2 Draw a picture of a storm.

THE GOOD SAMARITAN

Jesus told special stories to the people he met. They were called **parables**.

There was a road that went from **Jerusalem** to Jericho. Many people who walked along the road were attacked by robbers. Jesus told a parable about someone who was attacked on the road. He called the story 'The Good Samaritan'.

A Jewish man was walking along the road. Suddenly, he was attacked by some robbers. They left him badly hurt by the side of the road.

Later, a Jewish priest walked by. He saw the man, but he did not stop to help him. Then, another man (a **Jew**) walked by. He did not stop to help the man either. The next person to come down the road was a Samaritan. He was riding a donkey. He picked the Jewish man up and put him on the donkey.

The Samaritan took the man to the nearest town. He paid for someone to look after the injured man. Soon the man felt much better.

Jesus told people this story to teach a very important lesson. We should help everyone who needs our help, even if we don't know them. We should even help people we don't like.

IT'S A FACT

In the story of the Good Samaritan:

- The man attacked by the robbers was a Jew.
- The two people who passed by without stopping were Jews.
- It was a Samaritan who helped the man. The Jews and the Samaritans had not spoken to each other for over 300 years. This shows what a good man the Samaritan was. He stopped to help an enemy.

WHAT DO YOU THINK?

Imagine that you were the Samaritan. Would you have stopped to help the man?

THINGS TO DO

1. In our world there are many people who are not as well off as us. Here is a group of people who are not so well off as others. Who are they? Talk about what we could do to help them.
2. Ask your teacher to tell you about the 'Samaritans'. Find out how they got their name.

JESUS RIDES A DONKEY

Jesus and his **disciples** decided to go to **Jerusalem**. Jerusalem was a big, busy city. By this time, Jesus was very famous. He could have been rich. But he knew that money would not help him to do God's work. He could have ridden into Jerusalem on a horse, like a king. Instead he chose to ride into the city on a donkey. But people still treated him like a king.

Jesus sent two of his disciples to get a donkey.

The disciples put their coats on the animal. Jesus sat on the donkey. He rode into Jerusalem.

A strange thing happened. People started to put their coats on the road in front of the donkey. Other people cut branches down from palm trees and put them on the road.

The people knew that Jesus was the Son of God. They wanted to show how happy they were to see him.
The day that Jesus went into Jerusalem is called Palm Sunday.

 IT'S A FACT

- Every year Christians celebrate Palm Sunday. It is the Sunday before **Easter Day**.
- On Palm Sunday, Christians remember Jesus riding into Jerusalem on a donkey.
- Many churches hold a special procession on Palm Sunday. It is led by a donkey. Why do you think they do that?

THINGS TO DO

1. How did Jesus go into the city of Jerusalem? What did people put down in front of him?
2. Draw a picture of what happened when Jesus went into Jerusalem.

JESUS WASHES HIS DISCIPLES' FEET

Jesus tried to help and love everyone he met. It did not matter if they were rich or poor. He wanted to teach his **disciples** to do the same. Jesus and his disciples had been walking for a long time. They were very tired. Jesus poured some water into a bowl. He began to wash and dry his disciples' feet.

The disciples were shocked. Only the lowest servant washed other people's feet.
Peter told Jesus to stop. But Jesus would not stop.
Afterwards, Jesus spoke to his disciples.

He told them that he had washed their feet to help them and to show his love for them. It did not matter that it was a servant's job. He said that they must help and love all the people they met – even if they were the lowest servants. He told them about some ways to help people. They could:

Visit people in prison.

Give food and water to people who were hungry and thirsty.

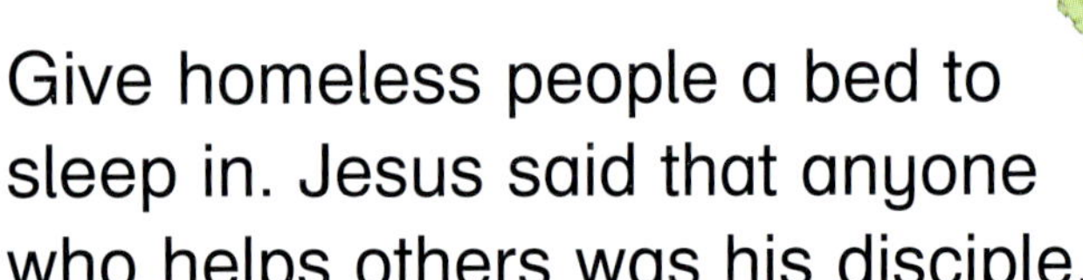

Give homeless people a bed to sleep in. Jesus said that anyone who helps others was his disciple.

IT'S A FACT

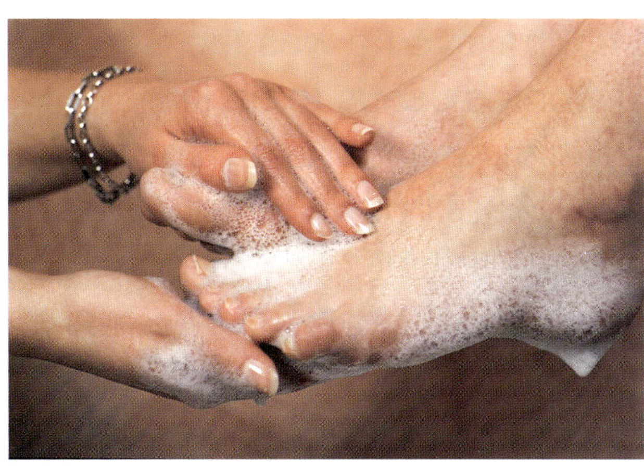

- **Palestine** was a very hot and dusty country.
- People wore sandals on their feet all the time.
- By the end of the day their feet were hot and dusty.
- Rich people had servants to wash their feet for them.

WHAT DO YOU THINK ?

Jesus washed his disciples' feet. Christians remember the day that he did this. They call it **Maundy Thursday**. In the past, on Maundy Thursday, kings washed their subjects' feet. Why do you think they did this?

THINGS TO DO

1. Draw two pictures that show you helping someone else. Talk about your drawings with the person sitting next to you. What have you drawn? Have you ever helped anyone in this way?
2. Imagine that the Queen walked into your classroom and started to wash everyone's feet. What would you say to her?

JESUS EATS HIS LAST MEAL

Jesus had many enemies. They did not believe he was the Son of God. They told the Romans that they wanted Jesus to be killed. Before the Roman soldiers came to kill him, Jesus wanted to make sure his **disciples** would not forget him. He sat down to eat supper with his disciples. He knew that it would be the last time he would eat with them.

He said that one of them would hand him over to the Roman soldiers. The disciples talked to each other. They did not think any of them would do such a terrible thing. Just then, Judas stood up and left.

Then, Jesus took some bread in his hands. He broke it into pieces. He ate it with his disciples.

After this, Jesus filled a cup with wine. Each disciple took a sip. He asked them to remember him when they ate bread or drank wine. This meant they would remember him for the rest of their lives.

Jesus stood up to go. He asked **Peter**, James and John, his best friends, to go with him. Jesus walked with them to a beautiful garden, called the Garden of Gethsemane.

Jesus spent the whole night in the garden. He prayed to God. He knew that he was going to die soon.

IT'S A FACT

- Holy Communion is the most important service in most churches.
- At this service Christians eat bread and drink wine.
- This reminds them of the Last Supper (Jesus' last meal).

THINGS TO DO

Look at the photograph.

1 Can you find Jesus?

2 How many disciples are there around the table?

3 Apart from bread, one other food is shown on the table. What is it?

JESUS DIES

Jesus was praying in the Garden of Gethsemane when the Roman soldiers came to take him away. His **disciples** were scared. They thought the soldiers might take them away too, so they ran away.

The soldiers took Jesus to see the **High Priest**, the Jewish leader. The High Priest said that Jesus had lied to the people by saying he was the Son of God. He said that Jesus would be punished for lying by being killed.

Then, Jesus was taken to see **Pontius Pilate**, an important Roman soldier. The High Priest had told Pontius Pilate what Jesus had done. But Pontius Pilate did not think Jesus should be killed. He did not know what to do.

Pontius Pilate asked the people who lived in **Jerusalem** what he should do.

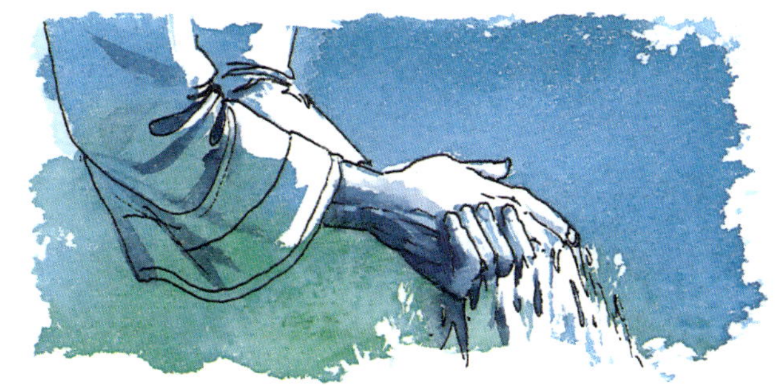

They said Jesus should be killed. Pontius Pilate called for a bowl of water. He washed his hands in front of the people. He wanted to show them that he did not agree with them.

Then, Jesus was taken away outside Jerusalem, to the top of a hill called Calvary. The soldiers made Jesus carry a big, heavy wooden cross up the hill. Then Jesus was nailed to the wooden cross. Soon, he was dead.

WHAT DO YOU THINK?

Two other men, who were robbers, died with Jesus. Do you think the disciples would have been killed with Jesus if they had not run away?

Do you think that Jesus was scared when he was on the cross?

THINGS TO DO

Pictures like these are found on the walls of many churches. Look at the pictures carefully. What is happening in each picture?

JESUS LIVES AGAIN

When **Jesus** died his **disciples** were very upset. They were also very scared. They were too scared to keep on teaching people about God, and helping them. They thought that the Romans might come and get them as well as Jesus. So they hid together in a room and bolted the door behind them. Later they heard an amazing story . . .

Mary Magdalene had been helped by Jesus. So she and a friend went to where Jesus was buried. Jesus was buried in a tomb. When they got to the tomb, it was open.

They looked inside the tomb. They saw a man dressed in white clothes. He looked like an **angel**. The body of Jesus was not there.

Mary saw someone standing outside the tomb. He looked like a gardener. She went to talk to him. She thought he might know where Jesus' body had gone. The stranger spoke Mary's name. She knew it was Jesus. He was alive.
Mary ran to find the disciples. She was so excited. They did not believe her story. Then, Jesus

spoke to them as well. Jesus told them that they should keep doing God's work. They should teach what he had taught, and they should tell people how he had died.

IT'S A FACT

- A long time ago, people were buried in tombs. You can see a tomb in this photograph.
- Tombs were often carved out of the rock.

- Christians believe that Jesus came back to life. They celebrate this on a special day each year, called **Easter Day**.

THINGS TO DO

1. Imagine that you are Mary Magdalene. How would you make the disciples believe that Jesus had come back to life? What would you say to them?
2. Do you eat Easter Eggs and Hot Cross Buns? Find out why we eat these things at Easter time.

MUHAMMAD GROWS UP

Muslims believe that a special baby was born in a town called **Makkah**, in Arabia, a long time ago. His name was **Muhammad**. They believe that **Allah** (God) sent Muhammad to earth to do some very special work.

Muhammad had a hard life when he was young. His father had died before he was born. His mother died when he was just six years old. Muhammad was brought up by his grandfather and uncle. He spent his days looking after the family's sheep on the hillside near his home.

Muhammad grew up to be a good man. He left home and went to work. He worked on a camel-train. A camel-train is a group of camels walking in a long line across the desert. The camels carry things on their backs.

After a few years Muhammad married the woman who owned the camel-train. Her name was **Khadijah**.

Muhammad and Khadijah were very happy together. They had six children.

IT'S A FACT

- Islam is a very old religion.

- The followers of Islam are called Muslims.
- When Muhammad was alive, camel-trains were used to carry things across the desert. They often carried wood and spices.

- Arabia is now called Saudi Arabia.
- Saudi Arabia is in a part of the world called the Middle East.

THINGS TO DO

Use this map to help you answer these questions:

1 In which country was Muhammad born?

2 What are the names of the two seas around Arabia?

3 What are the names of two towns in Arabia?

4 Which three towns were visited by the camel-trains?

MUHAMMAD AND THE BLACK STONE

In the middle of **Makkah**, there is a very special building. It is called the **Kaaba**. In the middle of one of the walls is a large **Black Stone**. When Muslims visit Makkah, the Kaaba is the first place they go to. They go there to kiss the Black Stone.

There is an old Muslim story that tells us how the Black Stone came to be put in the wall of the Kaaba. It tells us why Muslims believe that the Black Stone is so important.

A man called **Ibrahim** built the Kaaba. He had been sent to earth by God just like **Muhammad**. One day while he was working, he asked his son, Isma'il, to give him a stone to put in the wall. Isma'il bent down and picked up the Black Stone.

Muslims today visit Makkah. The first place they visit is the Kaaba. They kiss the Black Stone as they walk past.

Years later, when Muhammad was young, the Kaaba needed to be repaired. Many men worked together to repair it.

They had to take out the Black Stone. When it was time to put it back, they argued about who would do it.

They decided to let the first person to walk past the Kaaba next morning choose who would put the Black Stone back. That person was Muhammad.

The workers asked Muhammad to choose who would put the Black Stone back in place. But instead Muhammad put the Black Stone on a sheet. He asked everyone to take hold of the edge of the cloth, and they carried the Black Stone up to the Kaaba. Then Muhammad picked up the Black Stone and put it into its place. Everyone was happy because they had helped to put the Black Stone back. Everyone said that Muhammad was wise, and he became a hero in Makkah.

WHAT DO YOU THINK?

Do you think what Muhammad did was wise?

THINGS TO DO

1. In your own words, describe how Muhammad solved the problem of the Black Stone.
2. Imagine that you live in Makkah. You watch the Black Stone being put in place. Think of **one** sentence that describes what you see.

THE DREAMS OF MUHAMMAD

While **Muhammad** was growing up, he learned about **Allah**, and prayed to him. When Muhammad was older, he started to have dreams while he was praying. They were very special dreams. Muhammad used to go to pray in a small cave outside **Makkah**, called Hira.

Muhammad began to have special dreams. One night he saw the **Angel Gabriel** in the cave.

The angel told Muhammad to write down some special words. But Muhammad could not read or write. He had to tell his friends the words and they wrote them down for him. The angel spoke to Muhammad many times.

The words that the Angel Gabriel spoke to Muhammad are in the **Qur'an**. The Qur'an is the holy book that all **Muslims** read.

بسم الله الرحمن الرحيم
الحمد لله رب العلمين ۝ الرحمن
الرحيم ۝ ملك يوم الدين ۝ اياك نعبد
و اياك نستعين ۝ اهدنا الصراط
المستقيم ۝ صراط الذين انعمت عليهم
غير المغضوب عليهم و لا الضالين ۝

بسم الله الرحمن الرحيم
الم ۝ ذلك الكتب لا ريب فيه هدى
للمتقين ۝ الذين يؤمنون بالغيب و
يقيمون الصلوة و مما رزقنهم ينفقون ۝
و الذين يؤمنون بما انزل اليك و ما
انزل من قبلك و بالاخرة هم يوقنون ۝

IT'S A FACT

- The name of the Muslim God is Allah.
- Muslims still visit the cave of Hira.

THINGS TO DO

1. This book is the holy book that all Muslims read. What is it called?
2. How do you think Muhammad felt when he saw the Angel Gabriel? Talk to the person sitting next to you about it. Do you think that Muhammad was very scared? Would you have been?

MUHAMMAD VISITS HEAVEN

This story tells us why Muslims are taught to pray five times a day.

One night **Muhammad** rode from **Makkah** to **Jerusalem**, on the back of a horse with wings. Its name was Buraq.

When Muhammad got to Jerusalem, he went to a famous rock. It is still there today. A mosque has been built on the top of it.

Muslims try to pray five times every day. When they pray they kneel on a **prayer mat**.

At home

At work

In a **mosque**

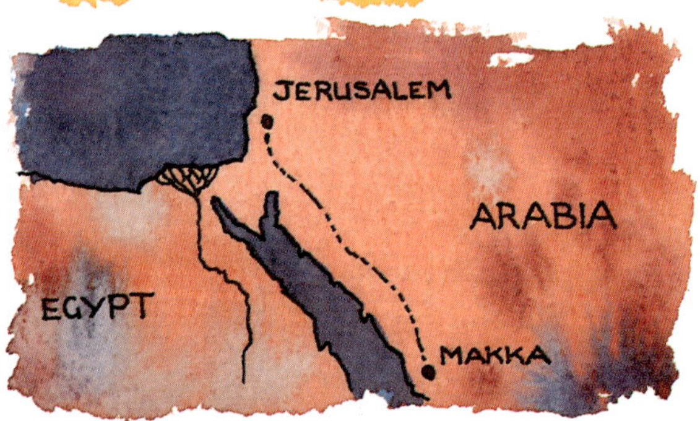

Muhammad went to the top of the rock. Suddenly, he was carried up into **heaven**. In heaven, he spoke to the **prophets**. They said that the people on earth should pray to **Allah** five times a day.

When Muhammad returned to earth, he told people about his visit to heaven. He told them what the prophets had said. Once a year, Muslims read about this in the **Qur'an**.

IT'S A FACT

- A prophet is a man or a woman who has been sent to earth by Allah.
- There have been many prophets.
- **Ibrahim**, **Jesus** and Muhammad were all prophets.

THINGS TO DO

The photograph shows a prayer-mat.

1. What would a Muslim use one of these for?
2. When might they use one?
3. Where might they use one?

THE GREAT JOURNEY

Muhammad had many enemies in **Makkah**. Some of them did not like what Muhammad told people about **Allah**, because they believed in other gods. Muhammad knew he had to leave Makkah. He got a message from the people of **Madinah**. They wanted him to go to Madinah and tell them about Allah. Muhammad decided to go.

Muhammad left Makkah in the middle of the night. His best friend, Abu Bakr, went with him.

Muhammad's journey from Makkah to Madinah is very important to **Muslims**. It is called the **Hegira** – the start of the **Islam** religion. In Madinah, Muhammad built the first **mosque** (where Muslims go to pray). There are now many mosques in the world. They all look like the first mosque.

Muhammad became the leader of the city of Madinah. The city went to war against Makkah, and won.

Muhammad did not kill his enemies. But he destroyed all the statues of the gods that they prayed to. Then, Makkah became a holy city for all Muslims.

IT'S A FACT

- Makkah is still the holy city for all Muslims.
- Every Muslim takes a journey to Makkah once in their life-time.
- This journey is called a 'pilgrimage'.

WHAT DO YOU THINK?

Why do you think that Muhammad left Makkah in the middle of the night to travel to Madinah?

THINGS TO DO

This photograph shows some Muslims making a pilgrimage to Makkah.

1. Look carefully at the photograph. What are the people wearing?
2. Draw a picture of a special journey that you have made.
3. Write two sentences about it.

MUHAMMAD DIES

After **Madinah** went to war against **Makkah**, **Muhammad** only went to Makkah once. He gave a famous speech to the people of Makkah. It is called his 'Farewell Speech'. In his speech, Muhammad told the people that they must do five things:

Pray to **Allah**

Pray five times every day

Go without food for one month each year.

Give money to the poor.

Visit the holy city of Makkah once in their lifetime

Muslims call these the 'Five Pillars'.

Then, Muhammad told the people that Allah would not send any more **prophets** to teach them. He was the last. They would have to teach other people and children about Allah.

A few months later Muhammad caught a fever and died. Abu Bakr, his best friend, told the people not to be sad. He said that Muhammad was dead but God lives for ever.

Muhammad was buried in the city of Madinah. His tomb is still there today.

A **mosque**, called the Prophet's Mosque, has been built over Muhammad's tomb. It has a green dome on top which can be seen from miles away.

IT'S A FACT

- The Prophet's Mosque is in Madinah.
- Muhammad is buried there.
- Abu Bakr is also buried there.

THINGS TO DO

1. Look at this drawing. Do you remember the five things that Muhammad told his followers to do? What were they?
2. These five things are called the 'Five Pillars' of Islam.

   Can you work out from this drawing why they are called that?

   Clue: What do the pillars in an old building do?

GURU NANAK GROWS UP

Guru Nanak started the **Sikh** religion. A **Guru** is a holy man or teacher. Nanak was the first Sikh Guru. He became a Guru when he was grown up.

Nanak was born in Pakistan in 1469. He was a very wise child. His school teachers soon decided they could not teach him anything.

Nanak was brought up to follow the Hindu religion. When he was ten years old, he should have taken part in a special service. All Hindu boys have to take part in this service. A special thread is placed around one of their shoulders. They wear it for the rest of their lives.

But Nanak said that he wouldn't do it. He said that it was not important to wear the thread. He thought it was more important to live a good life.

Nanak's family were very upset. They were all Hindus. After this, Nanak grew up like any other Hindu boy. When he was older, Nanak got married. He loved his wife very much.

For a long time, Nanak worked as a store-keeper. Then he gave up his job and moved to another town.

Each morning and evening Nanak sat outside. He sang hymns and thought about God. Soon, people started to come and sing and pray with him. More and more people came. Then, Nanak began to teach the people about God. He became a Guru.

IT'S A FACT

- A sacred thread is placed on every Hindu boy when he is ten years old.
- He has to wear it for the rest of his life.

WHAT DO YOU THINK?

Why do you think that Nanak's teachers could not teach him anything?

THINGS TO DO

This is Guru Nanak. Can you answer these questions?

1. What does the word 'guru' mean?
2. Who was the first Sikh Guru?
3. Where was Guru Nanak born?

GURU NANAK DISAPPEARS

In 1499, when **Guru Nanak** was thirty years old, something amazing happened to him. It changed his life.

Each morning, Guru Nanak went down to the river to wash. One day he disappeared. His friends and family were very worried about him. They looked everywhere for him, but they could not find him.

His friends and family thought that he had drowned. But Guru Nanak was not dead. He had gone to **heaven**. After some time, God told him to go back to earth. He told the **Guru** to spend the rest of his life telling people about God.

Three days later, Guru Nanak came back to earth. He began to teach people at once.
Guru Nanak told them to live good lives. It did not matter which religion they belonged to.

The Gurdwara

Sikhs go to a special building to worship God. It is called a **gurdwara**. There are lots of paintings on the walls of gurdwaras. They show the story of Guru Nanak's life.

THINGS TO DO

Many people believe in heaven. Make a list of all the things you think might be in heaven. When you have finished your list draw two of the things.

GURU NANAK ON THE MOVE

Guru Nanak decided that he must tell more people about God. So, he left his family and set off across the country. He stopped and told people about God wherever he went.

Guru Nanak took two friends with him. One was called Mardana. He played music. He sang what Guru Nanak said. This helped people to remember what the **Guru** told them. Guru Nanak's other friend was called Bala. He sat next to the Guru and waved a fan to keep him cool.

Soon, many people wanted to become **Sikhs**. Guru Nanak decided to live with a group of them. He built a village to live in. It was near a river.

People came from all over the country to see Guru Nanak. They sat with him early in the morning and late at night. They thought about God together. They sang hymns with the Guru. They listened to what he said.

Some Sikhs cooked food and looked after the visitors. They all cooked in the same kitchen. They enjoyed washing up together.

IT'S A FACT

- Sikhs go to a gurdwara to pray.
- Every gurdwara has a kitchen.
- Cooking a meal and eating it is a very important part of every Sikh service.

THINGS TO DO

Draw a picture of Guru Nanak teaching. Mardana and Bala should be in your drawing.

AFTER GURU NANAK

Guru Nanak was getting old. He had two sons. They both wanted to be the next **Guru**, but Guru Nanak was not sure that either of them would make a good Guru. He decided to test them.

There was a pile of wet, dirty grass in a field. He asked his sons to carry it. They said no. A young **Sikh**, Lehna, picked it up at once.

This made Guru Nanak think that his sons might be too proud to lead the Sikhs. But he set them another test.

He dropped a coin into a deep pool of cold, dirty water. He asked his sons to get it for him. They said no. Again, Lehna did what the Guru had asked. He jumped straight into the water and came up holding the coin.

That night Guru Nanak made up his mind. He asked Lehna to lead the Sikhs in his place. Then he died.

Lehna became known as **Guru Angad**. There were eight more Gurus after him. The tenth Guru did not choose anyone to follow him. He told the Sikhs that there would be no more Gurus. Instead, they should use the holy book, the **Guru Granth Sahib**, to teach them how to lead good lives.

IT'S A FACT

- **Amritsar** is a holy city for Sikhs.
- There is a beautiful Sikh temple in Amritsar in Pakistan.
- It is called the Golden Temple.
- Sikhs travel from all over the world to visit the Golden Temple.

THINGS TO DO

Say whether each of these sentences is true or false.

1. The first Sikh Guru was Guru Nanak. True or false?
2. Guru Nanak had one son. True or false?
3. The holy place for all Sikhs is Makkah. True or false?
4. Sikhs go to a gurdwara to pray. True or false?
5. The holy book of Sikhs is called the Guru Granth Sahib. True or false?
6. The Golden Temple is in Amritsar. True or false?

KEYWORDS

ABRAHAM:	The father of all Jews.
ALLAH:	The name for God in Islam.
AMRITSAR:	The Sikh holy city.
ANGEL:	A special messenger sent by God.
ANGEL GABRIEL:	The angel who appeared to Mary and also to Muhammad.
BAPTISM:	When babies or adults become Christians they are dipped in water.
BETHLEHEM:	The village where Jesus was born.
BLACK STONE:	The large stone set in the wall of the Kaaba in Makkah.
DEVIL:	The evil power who tried to make Jesus do bad things.
DISCIPLES:	Jesus' special friends.
EASTER DAY:	The day when Jesus came back to life.
EXODUS:	When the Jewish slaves left Egypt.
GURDWARA:	Where Sikhs go to pray.
GURU:	A very holy teacher.
GURU GRANTH SAHIB:	The Sikh holy book.
GURU NANAK:	The Guru who started Sikhism.
HEAVEN:	The place where God lives.
HEGIRA:	Muhammad's journey from Makkah to Madinah.
HIGH PRIEST:	The most important Jewish leader.

HOLY SPIRIT:	God's special power.
IBRAHIM:	The Muslim name for Abraham.
ISLAM:	The religion started by Muhammad.
ISRAEL:	A country where Jews live.
JERUSALEM:	The capital city of Israel.
JESUS:	Mary and Joseph's son. He started the Christian religion.
JEW:	Someone who belongs to the Jewish religion.
JOSEPH:	Mary's husband and Jesus' father.
JUDAISM:	The religion of Jews.
KAABA:	The holy building in the middle of Makkah.
KHADIJAH:	The wife of Muhammad.
MADINAH:	The city where Muhammad went to escape from his enemies.
MAKKAH:	The holy city for all Muslims.
MARY:	Jesus' mother and Joseph's wife.
MAUNDY THURSDAY:	The day when Jesus washed his disciples' feet.
MOSES:	He led the Israelites out of Egypt.
MOSQUE:	Where Muslims go to pray to Allah.
MUHAMMAD:	The Prophet of Allah.
MUSLIM:	Someone who belongs to the religion of Islam.
NAZARETH:	The village where Jesus grew up.

PALESTINE:	The country where Jesus lived, now called Israel.
PARABLE:	A story that Jesus told to teach people about God.
PASSOVER:	A Jewish festival.
PETER:	The leader of the disciples of Jesus.
PONTIUS PILATE:	The Roman Governor of Palestine.
PRAYER-MAT:	A mat on which Muslims pray.
PROPHET:	A person sent by God.
QUR'AN:	The holy book for all Muslims.
SABBATH DAY:	A holy Jewish day.
SCRIBE:	A Jewish leader.
SIKH:	Someone who belongs to the Sikh religion.
SIKHISM:	The Sikh religion.
SYNAGOGUE:	Where Jews go to pray.
TEMPLE:	The building in Jerusalem where Jesus worshipped God.
TEN SAYINGS:	God's rules, given to Moses by God.
TORAH:	The first five books of the Bible.